The Philosophy of Schmütz

FOR MUZZA
& CLARA

Introduction: Schmütz, the Unexpected Philosopher

Schmütz is not your typical philosopher. She is a one-eyed cat, a cosmic enigma, and an agent of truth wrapped in fur. She does not write essays or give lectures. She purrs. She stretches. She judges. And in doing so, she reveals what most humans spend lifetimes chasing. Her life is a testament to a simple but profound truth: **existence is miraculous, and it is best lived on one's own terms.**

Why a cat? Because cats do not pander. They do not seek validation, nor do they concern themselves with the expectations of society. They walk their own paths—sometimes with grace, sometimes with chaos, but always with authenticity. Schmütz, in particular, has mastered this art. She sees the world through a singular lens—quite literally. And yet, her vision is more expansive than most. She sees what others miss, lives in the present with total awareness, and refuses to be anything other than exactly who she is.

This book is not (entirely) about idolizing a cat. It is about what we, as flawed and overthinking humans, can learn from one. Schmütz has no grand theories to propose. She does not need to prove her worth. She simply exists, and in doing so, she shows us the way to **freedom, contentment**, and **unapologetic, radical self-acceptance.**

Through her actions and habits—some hilarious, some deeply wise—Schmütz offers us a perspective foreign to the overcomplicated, overanxious human mind, even though its essence is as old as existence itself. One that is simpler, truer, and infinitely more joyful. In an age of endless self-help guides, maybe the purest wisdom comes from someone who doesn't give a damn about them. Welcome to **The Philosophy of Schmütz.**

CHAPTER 1

Not All Cats Love Boxes: The Danger of Assumptions

The Schmütz Story

For centuries, the world has perpetuated a blatant falsehood: *All cats love boxes.* Science backs it, the internet is filled with proof, and, yet, Schmütz exists as a defiant contradiction. Schmütz does **not** love boxes. In fact, she regards them as **noisy, unpredictable horrors** that must be avoided at all costs.

I first noticed this when she would mysteriously vanish the moment I stepped inside carrying a package. Eventually, I realized it wasn't just any package—it was specifically when I carried a **box** or anything that could be mistaken for one. Curious, I decided to put this to the test. One day, I waited until she was present before opening a package, thinking if she saw the box being handled gently, she'd learn that it posed no threat. The moment I made that first *tear* of cardboard, Schmütz **skidded across the floor in sheer panic** and disappeared under the bed.

Determined to prove that boxes were harmless, I presented her with an empty one—silent, unmoving, and entirely innocent. Schmütz took one glance and said, *Absolutely the eff not.* The only time she will ever go near a box is when it is **sitting alone** and I am **nowhere near it.** I can only conclude that Schmütz does not distrust boxes themselves—**she distrusts me with boxes.**

I once tried to **trick** her into engaging with one, placing a treat inside, thinking her love of snacks would override her suspicion. She took the treat, but the moment the box shifted, even slightly, she **bolted.** It wasn't about what was inside; it was about **the box's very nature.** And when I used cardboard in the garden as a base layer, channeling my inner Rebel

Gardener? The moment I moved it, Schmütz took one look, decided I was engaged in a deeply suspicious act, and darted inside, peering at me from behind a cracked door as if I had personally betrayed her in ways she couldn't yet articulate.

If Schmütz were called to the witness stand, she would deliver scathing testimony in favor of banning boxes under anti-terrorism laws. She has made her position clear, and at this point, I have stopped trying to change her mind.

Some things are simply non-negotiable. Schmütz has made it certain that she doesn't owe me or anyone else a performance. Neither do you.

The Schmütz Philosophy

Purr-sonal Truth: No Boxes Required
Forget the world's cookie-cutter checklist—you're writing your own rulebook, one quirky win at a time. Here's a little Schmützy strategy when the pressure mounts:

No, Thank You: The Power of Rejecting What Doesn't Fit
The world may insist that all cats love boxes, but Schmütz has no interest in performing for the sake of expectation. She does not entertain what doesn't feel right to her, no matter how many others swear by it. You are allowed to do the same.

Opting Out is an Option
Schmütz has made it clear: she will not be coaxed, convinced, or lured into a situation that doesn't suit her—unless, of course, there's a particularly irresistible snack involved. Even then, she proceeds with extreme caution. The world will always try to hand you a box—an expectation, a path, a label. You do not have to step inside. But if you must endure brief discomfort, make sure the treat is actually worth it.

The Suspicious Gardener: Some Things Are Not Your Problem
Schmütz watches as I shift things in the garden—not with concern, not with judgment, but with the calm neutrality of someone who has far more interesting things to do. She chases a grasshopper, lets the wind ruffle her fur, and sprawls in the dirt without a care for whatever experiment I'm conducting. Not everything needs your input. You are allowed to enjoy your own sunshine while the world carries on around you—and some of life's greatest delights, like the warmth of the sun, the dance of the wind, and the endless amusement of a well-timed grasshopper, are still free.

CHAPTER 2

Paws, Adapt, Play: Learning to Roll With the Punches

The Schmütz Story

Schmütz's story in the lives of those who know and love her could have been very short. She was hours away from being just a fleeting glimmer—a tender presence born during, and soon after lost to, another harsh northeast Missouri winter. Found alone in Canton, Missouri on a freezing December day, she weighed just 1.2 pounds at six weeks of age—a fragile scrap of life barely clinging to existence. But from the moment I encountered her, I was already absorbing her quiet wisdom, and her tiny yet mighty purrs urged me to savor the present. Enduring the worst case of ear mites even the seasoned vets—experts in wrangling scruffy outdoor kitties—had ever seen, she looked like she was on her last thread. Her urine was tinged with blood—a sight that still makes my stomach twist—and she sneezed relentlessly, trying to rid herself of congestion, while her breathing remained raspy. The vets were gentle but realistic in preparing me for the heartbreak that she might not make it.

But Schmütz had other plans.

Blind and unable to smell, she had to learn the world in an entirely different way. I started by bottle-feeding her, and as she gained strength, I began placing tiny bits of food on her tongue—because she couldn't see or smell that it was meant to be eaten. In true Schmütz fashion, the moment the delicious tuna pâté hit her taste buds, the rest of it was toast. I quickly learned to withdraw my finger or risk an encounter with her razor-sharp teeth! In her defense, I, too, am like this when hungry. Honestly, I've bitten my own lip before—apparently confusing it for a spicy chicken sandwich—and that was when I wasn't even remotely starving.

Then one day, a friend pointed out that Schmütz was following the movement of my face when I talked to her. I wanted to believe it, but I didn't dare. Her right eye was still bulging—macabre, inflamed, and clearly beyond saving. But her left eye was beginning to heal. Day by day, the swelling eased, the tissue calmed, and slowly—almost impossibly—she began to see. But by then, Schmütz had already learned to navigate the world in her own way.

In time, her ears recovered from the harsh assault of ear mites, and now twitched with every curious sound. But her right eye, refusing to heal and causing her constant pain, had to go—along with her ovaries, in a single, decisive act of relief and renewal. Her left eye, permanently scarred from her early struggles, offers her a uniquely soulful view of the world, while the rest of her body has pulled together to keep her full of life and a playful spirit. Even her chronic respiratory condition—yet another lingering reminder of her tough start, leaving her with a bit of extra mucus—is just another quirky badge from her journey. Through every challenge, Schmütz lives joyfully, showing us that real strength comes not from perfection, but from embracing our scars and dancing to our own beat. She loves every moment of her life, proving that even after a rough beginning, life can be wonderfully worth living.

Adaptation wasn't a choice. It was her art form. She didn't just survive—she thrived. On her terms.

The Schmütz Philosophy

One Paw in Front of the Other
"Every journey of a thousand miles begins with a single step" (Lao Tzu). Not every day bursts with brilliance. Sometimes, just making it through is a win on its own. Every step forward is a quiet victory, a testament to your resilience and a reminder that progress begins with simply showing up.

Whisker Wisdom
Trust the small wins—even when they're hidden from sight. When things seem hopeless, fine-tune your whiskers—even if you don't see (or smell!) the wins at first. Pay attention to the things you *can* control, and trust that everything else will unfold the way it was meant to.

Cosmic Catnaps
Embrace the power of a well-timed pause to regain your energy. Ultimately, life is a cosmic dance of flexibility and trust. Sometimes, the strongest move is to pause, focus on recharging, and let your energy build for the next leap forward.

CHAPTER 3

The Sunbeam Doctrine: Boundaries and Self-Respect

Not everything requires a reaction. Sometimes, the best response is to stay in your sunbeam or find a new one.

The Schmütz Story

Schmütz loves a good sunbeam. When she finds one, she melts into it, stretching out luxuriously, absorbing every drop of warmth like it was placed there just for her. It is her personal moment of bliss—until a human enters the scene, disrupting her grand display of feline serenity.

Approach her gently, call her name with love, and she may grace you with a slow blink or a soft meow. Get a little sweeter with your tone—"I lub you sooo much, my little Schmützyy"—and she might even roll over to show her magnificent *belleh*, paw at her face, and let you in on the secret joy of her warmth.

But there is a fine line.

Push too far, try to touch her before she's ready, or disrupt her peace jarringly, and she will simply remove herself—no dramatic exit, no grudge, just a smooth and effortless relocation to somewhere less complicated. Schmütz does not explain. She does not negotiate. She does not beg for understanding. She enforces. The world will adjust.

Even the ones who know her best have to tread lightly. When I come back from a trip and rush in too quickly, I get the familiar hiss—not out of spite, but as a gentle but firm reminder that trust, like sunbeams, must be eased into. After all, when someone disappears and then pops back in, it's only fair to wonder why. Love and respect? Those take time and space to really settle in.

The Schmütz Philosophy

Sunbeam Serenity

Know when to bask and when to bail.

A sunbeam isn't just a patch of light—it's a moment of peace. Schmütz knows when to stretch out and absorb all the warmth the world has to offer, but she also knows when to walk away and find a quieter spot. True serenity comes from knowing when to stay and when to slip away, quietly maintaining your personal space.

Slow Blink Truth

Trust takes time to build and nurture.

Schmütz knows that love doesn't mean unending access. When you've been away, it's okay to let things settle before diving back in. Trust grows slowly, and the most loving thing is to let it unfold at its own pace.

Hiss of Wisdom

Boundaries are love in motion.

A soft hiss isn't anger—it's a gentle reminder that respect must go both ways. Schmütz knows that love isn't about losing yourself. Sometimes, even love needs room to breathe. It's okay to ask for space, and it's okay to step back when you need to.

CHAPTER 4

The One-Eyed Perspective: Seeing What Others Miss

The Schmütz Story

Schmütz sees the world differently—literally. But does she dwell on it? Absolutely not. She struts through life as if she were granted an exclusive, high-definition filter the rest of us can only dream of. As a kitten, she was fully blind. The world, as far as I could tell, was an endless stretch of darkness for her, but she never acted lost. Instead, she listened. She learned to follow my voice, attuning herself to presence where others might have sensed only emptiness. She mapped her surroundings through sound, through vibrations, through something deeper than sight.

But her process wasn't foolproof. Let's just say the baseboards won that round. Schmütz, however, was truly unbothered by the setback. And when one eye healed while the other faded, she didn't hesitate—she just adjusted. Schmütz never sat in grief for what was changing. She never pitied herself, never looked back. She made the most of what remained, because to her, there was no other way.

Even now, with her one eye, Schmütz notices what others miss—the small, the subtle, the slightly suspicious. She perceives not just what is obvious, but what is hidden, what is felt rather than seen.

And maybe that's the real difference. Humans get caught up in comparisons, in what should be, in what they lack. But Schmütz? She doesn't burden herself with *shoulds*. She exists fully in the world she has, in the body she has, in the moment she is in. Her world isn't lacking—it's alive, rich with details most of us don't even think to notice. Schmütz doesn't see what's missing. She sees what matters. What if we did the same?

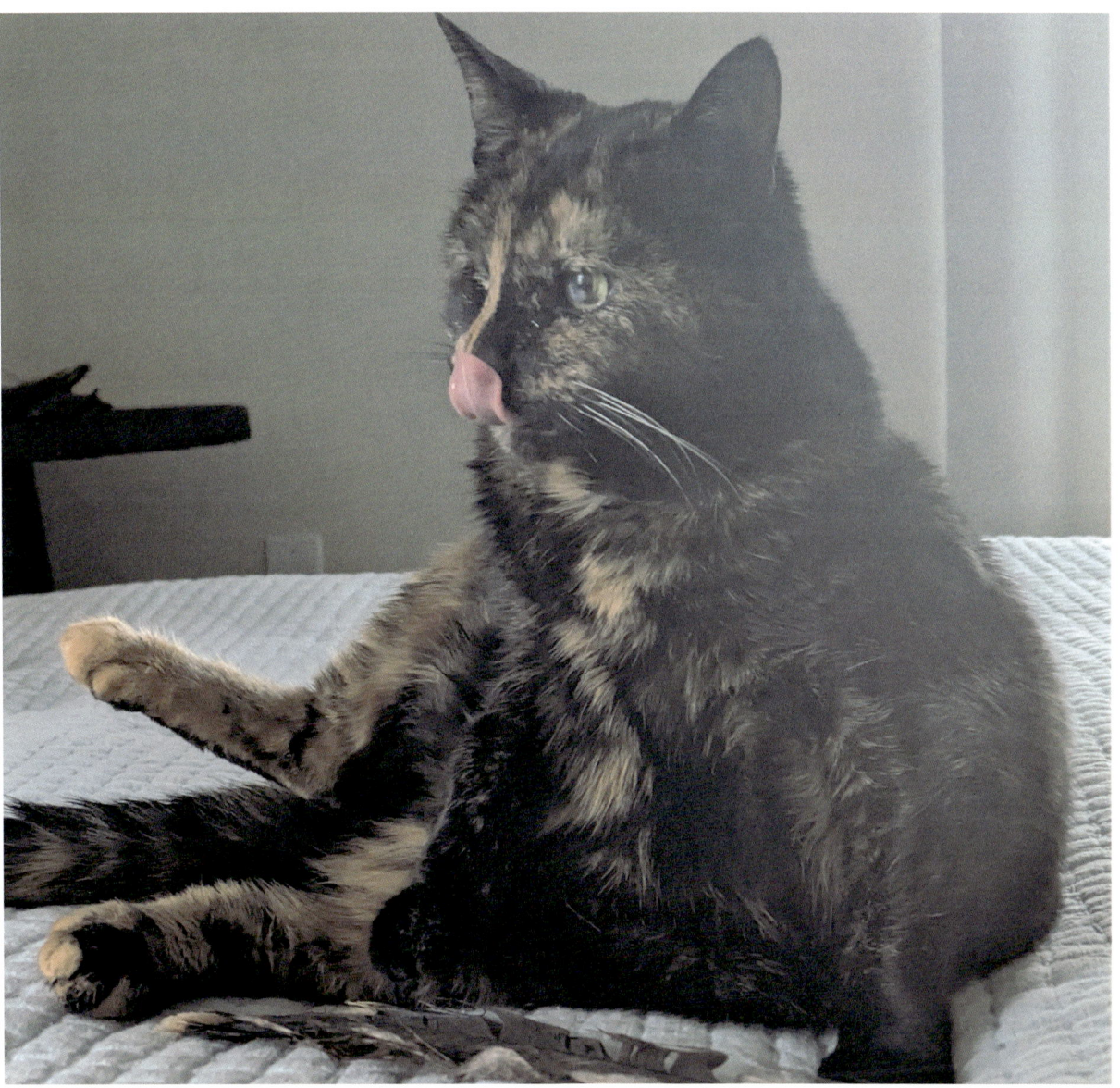

The Schmütz Philosophy

Adaptation Over Absence
Loss doesn't define you—adjustment does. Schmütz never dwelled on what was missing; she just kept moving. Life isn't about what you lack but how you work with what you have.

The Power of a Singular View
It's not about better or worse—it's just different. Schmütz doesn't see the world like others do, but she doesn't need to. She navigates in her own way; no complaints, no comparisons. Maybe the trick isn't perfect vision—it's trusting what you *can* see.

Noticing the Unnoticed
Life moves fast, and it's easy to overlook the little things. But Schmütz? She soaks it in—the flicker in the grass, the shimmer in the shadows, the sound her turkey feather toy makes when I rustle it, the quiet magic in the everyday. Take moments throughout the day to look out the window. Or maybe step outside. There's more to see than you think.

See With What You Have
Grief and loss are part of the ebb and flow of life. Give yourself time to mourn if you need it—but don't linger in guilt for moving forward. Schmütz never got stuck in what was lost—she adjusted, trusted, and kept going.

CHAPTER 5

The Schmütz Code of Social Energy: You Are Not Entitled to Me

The Schmütz Story

Schmütz is not human—but as a cat, she might as well be. Like all of us, she is a little bit yin, a little bit yang, adapting as life shifts around her. She does not dwell on what's lost, but that doesn't mean she never felt it. She just knows that presence matters more than absence, and that life, above all else, moves forward.

And Schmütz? She moves on *her* terms.

Schmütz does not suffer fools—or uninvited guests. She's not rude—just uninterested. Not every interaction deserves her purr. Not every knock gets a welcome. Schmütz doesn't do social niceties just to be polite. If she wants to be near you, she'll let you know. If not? She'll leave the room without so much as a glance.

It's not personal. Or maybe it is. Either way, that's for her to know and you to find out. She owes no explanation.

Enter Thylvethter (or, as we call him, "Thilly")—the neighborhood stud. Handsome, strong, a bird-capturing champion, and by all accounts, an absolute catch in the feline world. Schmütz had watched him from behind windows, tracking his movements with what I foolishly mistook for romantic interest. I assumed she was *intrigued*. Perhaps even *smitten*. So, when the opportunity arose for them to meet face-to-face, I opened a window (bug screen still in place, of course) and let them get acquainted.

Thylvethter approached, confident, assured. Schmütz annihilated him. No hesitation, no warning—ears flattened, tail fluffed,

unleashing a verbal onslaught so brutal I wondered whether to intervene or take cover. This was not flirtation. This was not coy resistance. This was an exorcism. Thylvethter did not need closure. He needed a priest.

Fast-forward a few summers. By then, Schmütz had grown bolder, stepping outside with me to bask in the sun like the tiny queen she is. And what did she do when she saw Thilly strolling back to his house? She confidently reminded him that her initial rejection was *not* up for renegotiation. And by "reminded," I mean I had to drag her, screaming, back inside before things got physical.

This was not a one-time rejection. This was a Royal Decree.

Schmütz has a rule: **you are not entitled to her energy.** Access is a privilege, not a right. She does not humor. She does not indulge. She does not explain.

She is, after all, a cat. But honestly, that's just good policy.

The Schmütz Philosophy

Selective Purring
You don't have to harmonize with every frequency. Some connections are effortless, like a sunbeam on fur. Others feel like trying to nap on a pile of pinecones—uncomfortable, unnatural, and not worth the effort. Schmütz doesn't force what isn't meant to be, so why should you?

Energetic Flow
Energy is a resource, not an obligation. Schmütz moves toward what nourishes her and away from what drains her, without guilt or hesitation. She does not fight against the current—she simply redirects her flow. The same choice is available to you.

Royal Decree
Not every presence deserves your presence. Just because the world finds someone impressive doesn't mean you must as well. Schmütz understands this. Kindness can be given freely, but access is something else entirely. And if the vibe isn't right, no amount of admiration will change that.

CHAPTER 6

The Myth of More: Why Schmütz Chooses Her Regular Food

The Schmütz Story

Schmütz is not easily seduced by novelty. While some cats chase after the latest gourmet treat or a fresh brand of kibble, Schmütz remains steadfast in her preferences. She knows what she likes, and she sees no reason to change just because something new is presented to her.

More than once, I have placed a gourmet offering in front of her, something extravagant, human-grade, and expensive. She will inspect it, acknowledge its existence, and then walk away, unimpressed. Then, with quiet certainty, she returns to her regular food—the one she has eaten for years, the one she trusts.

This is not stubbornness. This is wisdom. Schmütz is not interested in **more for the sake of more.** She is not tricked by flash or excess. She understands that satisfaction comes not from endless options but from knowing what works for you and sticking with it.

The Schmütz Philosophy

The Illusion of Novelty
Schmütz knows not everything is worth pursuing. She takes a look, considers, and if it doesn't feel right, she simply walks away—unrushed, unconcerned, and perfectly content with what she already has.

The Contentment Principle
Schmütz doesn't search for happiness because she recognizes that it's already here. She knows fulfillment isn't found in looking for

more, but in appreciating what already exists. A full bowl means nothing if it isn't what you truly want.

The Wisdom of What Works
Schmütz doesn't second-guess her choices or constantly search for an upgrade. She knows that, sometimes, the best thing to do is let what works keep working. Not everything needs fixing. Not everything needs effort. Some things are already enough.

CHAPTER 7

Endure When You Must, Avoid When You Can: The Schmütz Approach to Struggle

The Schmütz Story

Schmütz is no stranger to discomfort, but she is a master of discernment. She knows when to push through and when to walk away. She does not suffer needlessly, nor does she endure for the sake of endurance. Strength, in her world, is not measured by how much you tolerate—it's in knowing what's worth tolerating.

Take rain, for example. Some days, if she's outside soaking up the moment and a drizzle begins, she'll tolerate the wetness. She flicks the droplets off her whiskers, gives the sky a moment to reconsider, and presses on. Other days, if the first drop so much as grazes her fur, she's gone. No debate. No internal struggle. Just an immediate and unwavering exit. The difference? Her mood, her priorities, her choice.

She applies this same wisdom elsewhere. Vet visits, nail trims, the occasional indignity of being picked up or administered revolting anti-hairball grease bombs—these things must be endured. She does not like them, but she gets through them. Because some struggles are necessary. But when a struggle is not? Schmütz does not hesitate. She removes herself with the same certainty she applies to everything else.

We humans, on the other hand, love to make things harder than they need to be. We mistake suffering for strength, thinking resilience is about how much discomfort we can endure. Schmütz does not share this belief. She does not stay in the rain just to prove she can handle it, nor does she sit in discomfort for the sake of appearances. She knows what many of us do not: Some struggles are inevitable, but many are entirely optional. And if you can walk away from the pointless ones? Do it.

The Schmütz Philosophy

The Freedom of Not Proving Yourself
Schmütz has nothing to prove. She doesn't wear struggle like a badge or make a spectacle of her endurance. She exists fully in her own decisions—no second-guessing. Strength is not a performance; it's the quiet confidence of knowing you don't need to convince anyone of it.

The Balance of Endurance
Neither is strength about gritting your teeth through everything—it's in knowing when to exit with ease. Schmütz does not waste time explaining why she's done with something. She endures what she must, leaves what she can, and never wastes time looking back.

The Reality of Struggle
Some struggles are unavoidable—the things you'd rather skip but can't. Schmütz tolerates them, though not without protest, and moves on. She does not replay, relive, or retell the discomfort. She shakes it off, flicks a paw, and returns to whatever makes life good.

CHAPTER 8

Solitude Without Loneliness: The Schmütz Balance

The Schmütz Story

Schmütz enjoys attention—but only on her terms. She demands to go outside, then come back in, then back out again, announcing each transition with a series of meows that stretch longer and become more elaborate, as if composing an opera of impatience. She insists on playtime, selecting her preferred toy for the occasion—a turkey feather, a well-worn stick—making it clear that engagement is not optional. And when it comes to affection, she decides when and how it happens. And yet, she is not a loner. She enjoys company—always on her own schedule.

She exists alongside me, sometimes simply being in the same room, content in shared space, other times making her presence known with a sharp chirp or an unblinking stare that translates roughly to *You have a job to do, and that job is to entertain me*. If I leave, she notices. If I return, she acknowledges. But while she commands attention when she wants it, she does not crumble without it. Schmütz understands the art of solitude without loneliness.

She enjoys her independence but is also deeply connected. She does not cling, nor does she self-isolate—she simply is. She will rest nearby, attuned to the quiet rhythms of life, listening, absorbing, engaging without demanding. She takes comfort in shared space rather than closeness, in knowing companionship exists without the need to possess it. Schmütz reminds us that connection does not mean attachment, and solitude does not have to mean isolation. Balance isn't something to chase—it's something that settles naturally when you let it.

The Schmütz Philosophy

The Fullness of Solitude
Being alone and being lonely are not the same. Schmütz moves through life on her own terms, finding peace in her own company. She does not seek constant validation—she simply exists, content in the presence of herself.

The Quiet Connection
You don't have to constantly engage to feel connected. Schmütz teaches us that companionship isn't measured in words or gestures but in comfort. Humans panic over unanswered texts. Schmütz will sit next to you in total silence for hours, completely at peace.

The Space Between Togetherness
Connection isn't about constant closeness—it's about trust. Schmütz moves freely, knowing she can step away without losing her place. **Love** doesn't demand constant proof—it simply is.

CHAPTER 9

The Mirror is Just a Tool: Self-Perception, Schmütz-Style

The Schmütz Story

Schmütz acknowledges mirrors, but she does not obsess over them. She has looked, she has seen, and she has moved on. Unlike humans, who stand before their reflections critiquing every perceived flaw, Schmütz understands that a mirror is nothing more than a tool—a passing moment of recognition, neither a source nor a measure of self-worth.

She may glance at herself occasionally, a flicker of curiosity followed by a slow blink of approval before carrying on with her day. When she grooms near a mirror, it is not to adjust or perfect, but simply because she feels like grooming. Her self-image is not something to be managed or scrutinized; it is something she inhabits naturally, without question. Schmütz exists in a state of **uncomplicated self-acceptance**.

Schmütz does not seek validation from her reflection, nor does she let it dictate her mood. She is as she is, whole without comparison. To her, a mirror is no more significant than a puddle or a pane of glass—something to notice, not something to consult. She does not need a reflection to confirm who she is. She simply exists, at peace with herself, as we all could be.

The Schmütz Philosophy

The Lightness of Looking
A mirror offers a glimpse, not a verdict. Schmütz looks, acknowledges, and moves on—because her sense of self isn't up for debate. When you build a life filled with love, joy, and presence, your reflection becomes just another passing moment—not a measure of your worth.

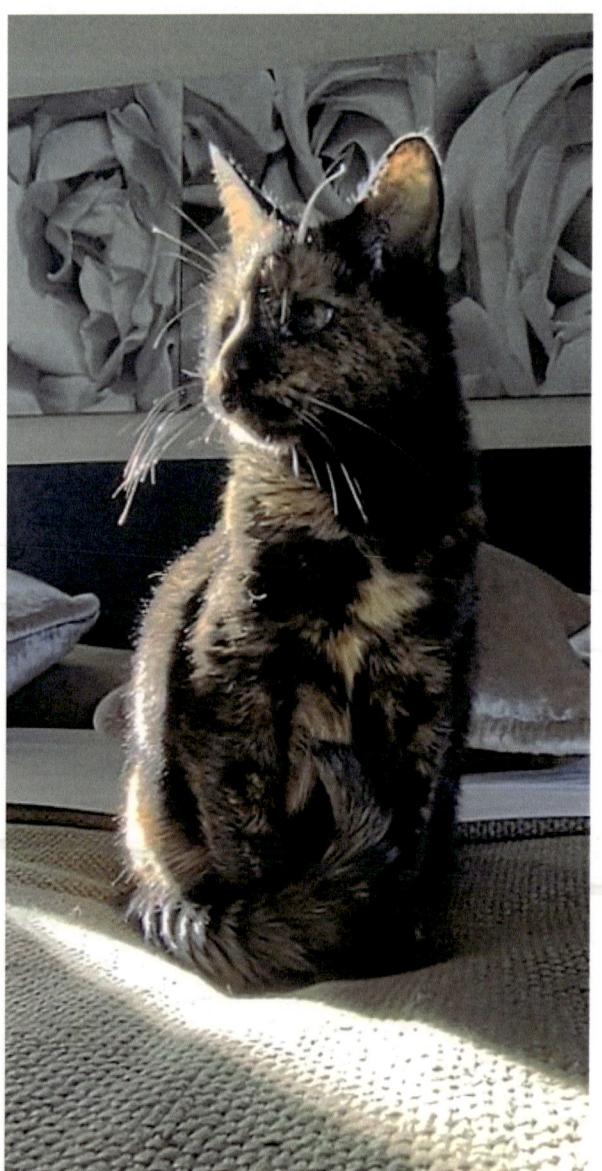

The Simplicity of Self-Love
Schmütz doesn't tweak, filter, or obsess—her joy comes from being, not appearing. True self-acceptance isn't about whether you like what you see, but about loving yourself so completely that it no longer matters.

The Unshaken Reflection
Schmütz sees herself without attachment. Mirrors come and go. Reflections change. Her contentment does not. When you cultivate presence, joy, and love for who you are beyond the surface, no reflection—good or bad—can take that away.

CHAPTER 10

The Art of Ease: Living Without Force

The Schmütz Story

Schmütz has never rushed a single thing in her life. She stretches when she wakes, eats when she's hungry, rests when she's tired. She does not question these instincts, nor does she fight against them. There is no guilt in her stillness, no urgency in her movement. She does not measure the value of her day by how much she has accomplished. She simply exists, fully and without hesitation.

She accepts what is given to her—a warm sunbeam, a familiar touch, a quiet place to nap—without questioning whether she deserves it. When she plays, she plays with her whole body. When she sleeps, she sleeps without tension. She does not resist the natural rhythms of life.

The world often tells us we must earn our rest, prove our worth, and justify our joy. Schmütz does none of these things. She knows there is nothing to earn, nothing to prove. She does not grip onto life, nor does she shrink from it. She allows herself to move as she is meant to move—without force, without doubt.

In the summer garden, the asparagus returns each year, taller, wilder, unrecognizable to most who pass by. No one asks it to grow, yet it does, stretching toward the light, bending with the breeze, existing without explanation. It is what it is, and that is enough. Schmütz, sprawled long in the dirt beside it, as if she, too, were planted there with no particular agenda beyond existing, belongs just as effortlessly—present, unbothered, alive in the only moment that matters: this one.

One day, the garden will change. The asparagus will return until, one year, it does not. Schmütz will bask in the sun until, one day, she won't. And though this thought stings me as a human, she does not carry that sorrow. She does not wait for endings—she simply lives. Maybe she does not know that her time is limited, or maybe she does. Maybe, in her own quiet way, she understands something we struggle to accept: The **Love** she leaves behind will linger—soft, steady, and entirely unbothered by time.

And even as this truth breaks my heart, I know this is the best outcome. Because the thought of leaving her first, of her searching for me in places I no longer am—that is something I could not bear.

You are allowed to do the same. You are allowed to rest before you are exhausted, to receive without justification, to move at the pace that feels right. You are allowed to live without force.

The world will go on. The garden will grow. And somewhere—if only in my heart, and perhaps now, yours—Schmütz will always be stretched long in the sun, exactly as she was meant to be.

The Schmütz Philosophy

The Ease of Enough:
Schmütz does not chase. She takes what is offered—a soft spot to nap, a warm patch of light—and moves on when it no longer feels right. Enough isn't something to seek; it's something to recognize.

Sprawl Without Apology:
Schmütz doesn't shrink herself to be smaller within her own spaces. When the moment calls for it, she sprawls, long and content, taking up space without explanation. It is her space to be taken. Live like that. You are allowed to exist fully, without shrinking to fit anyone's expectations, without diminishing yourself because someone thinks you should, or because you feel like you should to please another person.

The Quiet Acceptance of Cycles:
Like all of creation, the birds, the bees, the flowers, Thylvethter, and the asparagus will return until, one day, they won't. Schmütz will bask in the sun until she doesn't. This is the way of all things. But today? She is here. And that is enough. Yesterday is gone and tomorrow is not guaranteed. **Be here, now—because that is everything.**

Recognizing Your Schmütz

Watching Schmütz didn't change everything—but it stirred something. A pause. A question. A shift I didn't have words for at the time. Just a feeling that maybe the quiet moments—the ones we barely notice—are the ones that matter most. Maybe you've felt it too—that same Schmütz energy, not just in your cats, but in your people.

Maybe it's your relative with the laugh that's just a little too loud and the timing that's just a little bit off.

Or your sweet old friend who ended up in the nursing home—hair askew, repeating old stories, the polish of her past softening with time.

Or the one who always asks to hang out at your place because theirs isn't quite ready. You get it. Because it's never really about the place anyway. You have fun wherever you are, whatever you're doing together.

Or maybe they're running around your living room right now, crayon in hand, paying no mind to the concept of "paper only," because the wall had a lot more space for self-expression.

They're not aiming to inspire, not trying to be examples. They're just showing up as themselves, unfiltered, honest, and beautifully human. And when we meet them with an open heart, we see something we know. Something we remember.

Maybe you didn't have a name for it before. But now? You do. They're a Schmütz.

And so are you.

Welcome to the club.

The Schmütz in you recognizes the Schmütz in them. And that recognition? That's **Love**. Quiet. Certain. Enduring. Without Love, none of us would be here. No stories to tell. No laughter,

no tears, no hands reaching for one another in the dark. Without **Love**, there would be no Schmütz. And maybe, without the love she gave and allowed me to give, I wouldn't be here to share this at all. That wild, exquisite force of love—the kind that lifts us in joy and aches through us in grief. As with Schmütz, my Schmütz, your Schmütz, me, and you, as it was in the beginning, so shall it be in the end, because **Love is everything**.

We don't learn to love this way from billboards or self-help slogans. It's something we're born knowing. But somewhere along the way, we start believing that love needs to look a certain way. It gets repackaged as something watered-down—a love that comes from the mind, not the heart. But real love? It's softer and messier. Organic and divine. It's not something you measure. **It's something you feel**. And when we feel it, when we recognize it, we know that **Love** isn't about perfection. It's about presence.

If you're feeling curious about how to welcome more of that Schmütz energy into your own life—more ease, more presence, more unfiltered you-ness—here are a few gentle ways to begin. Think of them not as assignments, but as invitations. **Try what feels right. Leave the rest**—Schmütz would.

Schmützing About: Experiments in Living With Ease

Reading about Schmütz's way of life is one thing—**living it** is another. Consider these as gentle experiments, not assignments. **Try them. See how they feel. Leave what doesn't resonate.** Schmütz would never force it. What happens if you don't either?

The Sunbeam Challenge

Find your version of a sunbeam—a place, a moment, an activity that feels good just for the sake of feeling good. **No productivity, no "earning" it.** Just being. Sit with it, soak it in, and notice what happens when you let yourself exist in simple pleasure without narrating it, without proving anything, without looking for the next thing. **Just this moment. That's enough.** Schmütz is a master of sprawling across the bed like a Renaissance painting, basking in sunny warmth. Take a note from her—find your sunbeam, stretch into it, and see what happens when you just... let yourself enjoy it.

The Energy Audit

For the next few hours, notice where your energy naturally flows and where it drains. No need to fix anything—just observe. **What feels easy? What feels heavy?** If something depleted her, Schmütz would simply step away, no explanation needed. Try it. Even once. Even for five minutes. See what happens when you choose where your attention goes instead of letting it be taken. You might be shocked at how much time you spend **mentally entertaining things that aren't even paying rent**. Schmütz would never tolerate an energy squatter, and maybe there's something to that.

The "No" Recalibration

Schmütz doesn't overthink a "no." She doesn't write a novel of excuses or soften it with a thousand apologies. **She simply exits**. Next time you don't want to do something, practice a Schmütz-style no—short, clear, and guilt-free. No monologue, no justifying. Just a gentle, firm *no thank you*, followed by you going about your day. And if someone pushes? Give them *The Look*. You know the one. Schmütz does it best, but you'll get there.

The Appreciation Exercise

Schmütz doesn't chase more. She knows what she likes, and she sticks with it—not because she's stubborn, but because **not everything needs upgrading**. Take a moment to notice **what in your life already works**—an old sweater, a well-worn book, the same three songs on repeat. How does it feel to **choose what you already have and love** instead of reaching for something new just because it's there? Hint: This is probably better than impulse-buying another pair of socks you didn't need but somehow convinced yourself were life-changing. Schmütz would roll her eye at that one, and she'd be right.

The Mirror Reset

Next time you catch your reflection, try this Schmütz approach: **Acknowledge, blink, move on**. No assessing, no adjusting, no critiquing. Just a glance, a nod to yourself, and on to the next thing. Notice what shifts when you treat your reflection with the same casual, effortless acceptance Schmütz gives hers. After all, she's never once changed her fur pattern because the lighting was unflattering.

Conclusion: The Schmütz Way of Life

As far as I know, Schmütz has never read a self-help book, nor has she attended a single seminar on personal growth. Then again, I can't say for sure what she does when I'm not looking. Maybe she's been sneaking in TED Talks while I sleep. And yet, she moves through life with an ease, confidence, and sense of purpose that most humans spend decades trying to cultivate.

She does not force what isn't meant for her. She does not overthink what has already been decided. She does not apologize for existing exactly as she is.

She embraces what she loves without shame, removes herself from what does not serve her, and naps in a sunbeam whenever possible.

Perhaps the true secret to happiness isn't in constant striving, but in embracing life with the simplicity and certainty of a one-eyed cat who knows exactly who she is.

The Schmütz way of life is not about perfection, nor is it about endless improvement. It is about moving through the world with authenticity, self-respect, and a willingness to see beauty where others might miss it.

All that you need is within you. When you focus on healing yourself—on finding that inner joy and peace—it radiates outward in ways others can feel. Schmütz does not seek approval. She does not chase meaning. She simply is. And in being fully herself, she brings warmth to those around her.

Live fully, rest deeply, and trust that you are already enough.

And when you figure out how to do that, seriously, please let me know!

;) THE END ;)

From the Brink: Schmütz, Before Her Glow-Up

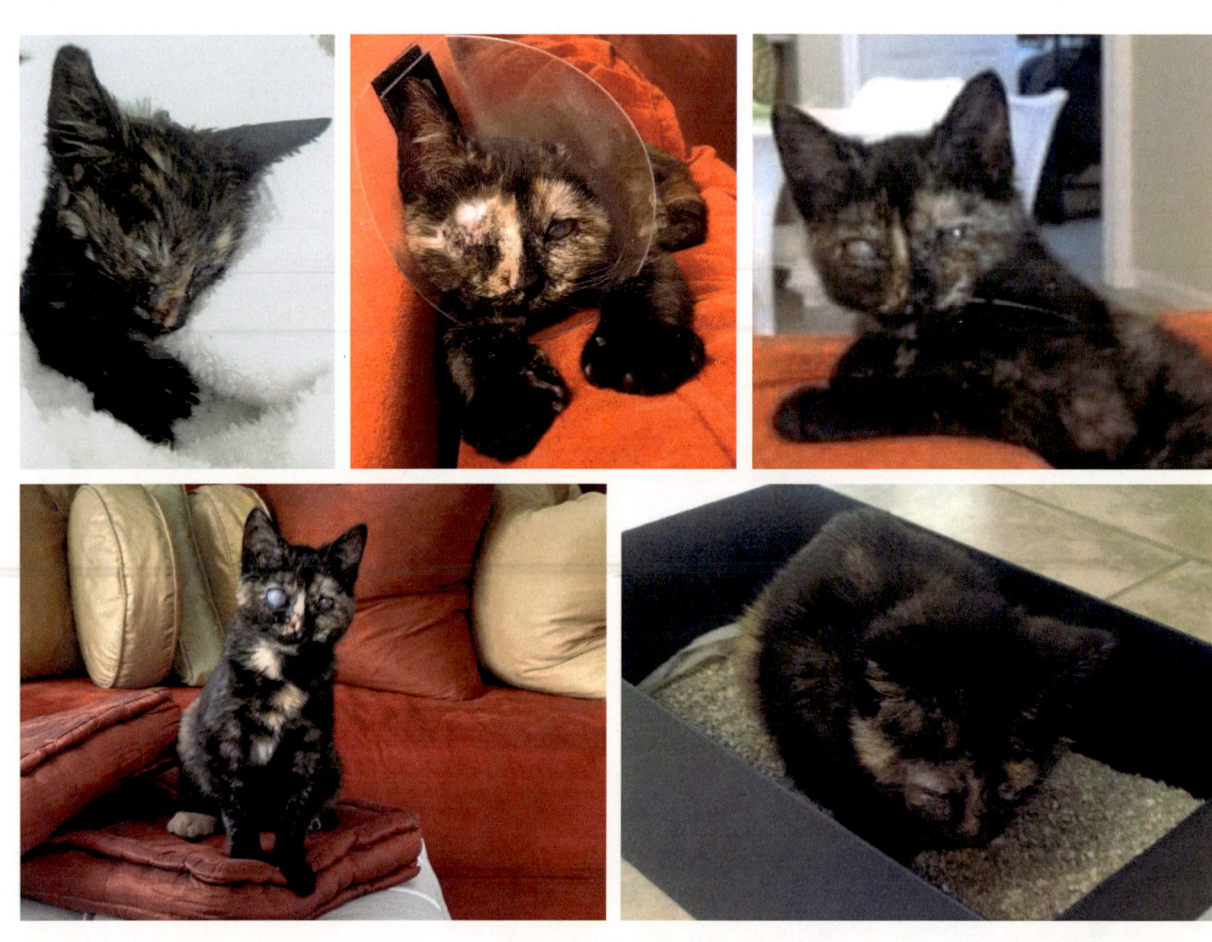

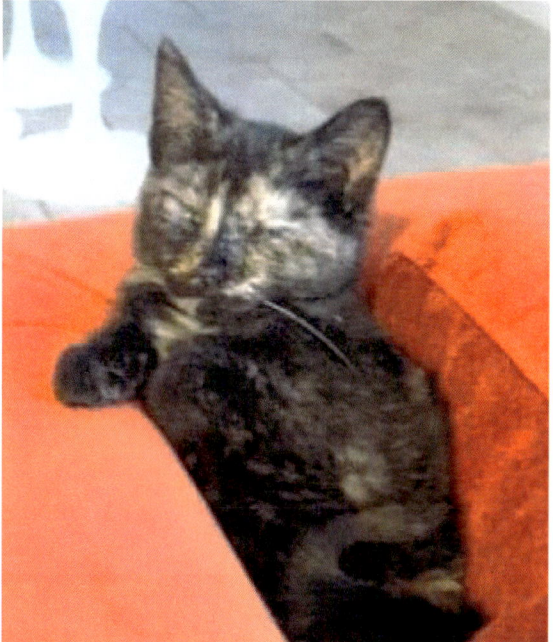

AUTHOR BIO

M. E. Seegulam is a Trinidadian-American biologist with degrees from Williams College and Washington University in St. Louis. He lives in rural Missouri with Schmütz, his one-eyed tortoiseshell cat who found him in the winter of 2015. This is their Midwestern queer love story—but probably not the kind you're used to.

Copyright © 2025 M. Esa Seegulam

All rights reserved. No part of this book may be reproduced by any means without the written permission of the author, except for short passages used in critical reviews.

Design and layout by Collette Sadler @collettesadler

ISBN Hardcover: 979-8-9993120-0-6
ISBN Paperback: 979-8-9993120-1-3
ISBN eBook (EPUB): 979-8-9993120-2-0

Want more
Schmütz
in your life?

Visit www.myschmutz.com
for a full line of Schmützified goodies.

www.ingramcontent.com/pod-product-compliance
Lightning Source LLC
Chambersburg PA
CBRC091934130526
44582CB00049B/184